John Crunden, John Taylor

The joiner and cabinet-maker's darling, or, Pocket director :

containing sixty useful designs, forty of which are gothic, Chinese,

mosaic, and ornamental frets, proper for friezes, imposts,

architraves, tabernacle frames, book-cases, tea tables, tea

John Crunden, John Taylor

The joiner and cabinet-maker's darling, or, Pocket director : containing sixty useful designs, forty of which are gothic, Chinese, mosaic, and ornamental frets, proper for friezes, imposts, architraves, tabernacle frames, book-cases, tea tables, tea

ISBN/EAN: 9783743612310

Printed in Europe, USA, Canada, Australia, Japan

Cover: Foto ©Thomas Meinert / pixelio.de

Manufactured and distributed by brebook publishing software (www.brebook.com)

John Crunden, John Taylor

The joiner and cabinet-maker's darling, or, Pocket director :
containing sixty useful designs, forty of which are gothic, Chinese,
mosaic, and ornamental frets, proper for friezes, imposts,
architraves, tabernacle frames, book-cases, tea tables, tea

Plate 1.

Mosaic Frets proper for Friezes.

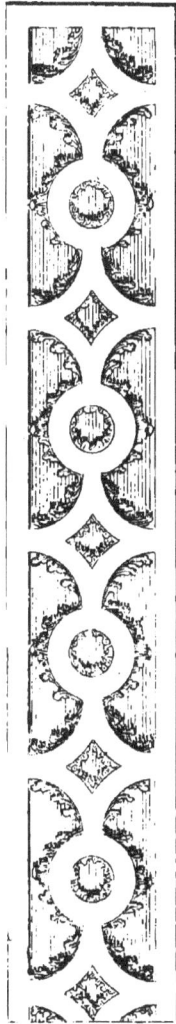

1.

Pl. 2.

Grand Mosaik Feel for a Frieze

Pl. 3.

Ornamental Frets for Friezes &c

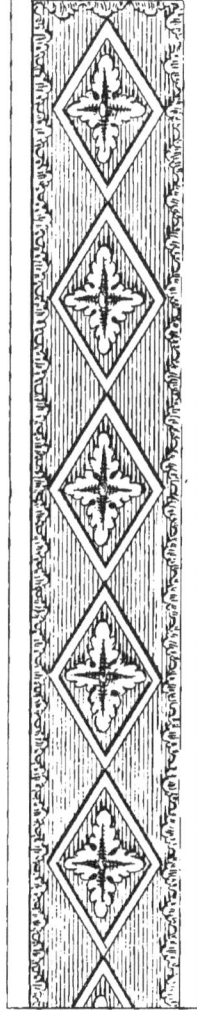

Pl. 4.

A Grand Gothic Fret

Pl.5.

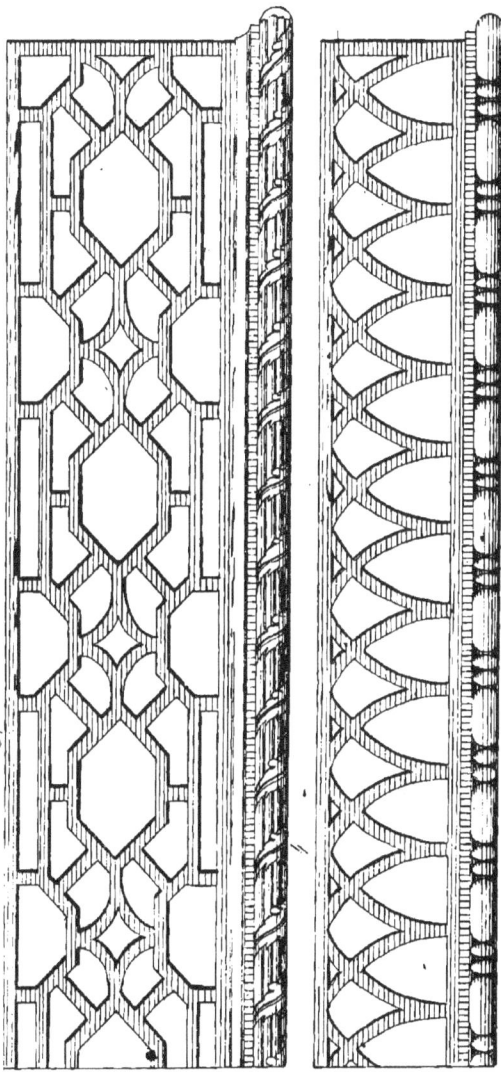

Two new Designs of Frets for Tea Stands

Pl. 6.

Two New Frets proper for Trays or Fenders

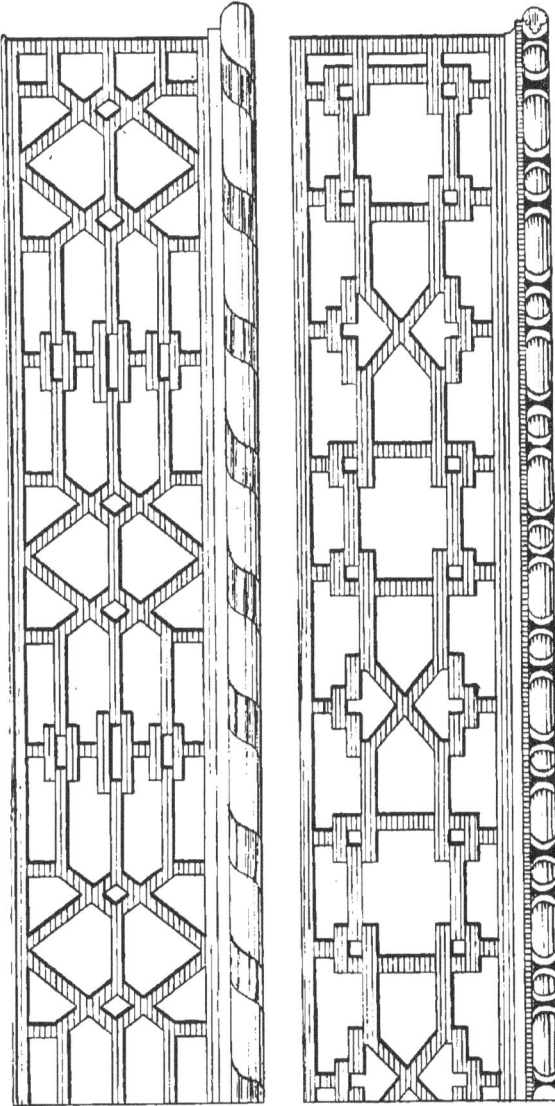

Pl. 7.

Two New Frets for Cabinet Makers &c

Pl.8.

Frets proper for Trays

Pl. 9.

Frets proper for Tea Stands, Trays and Fenders

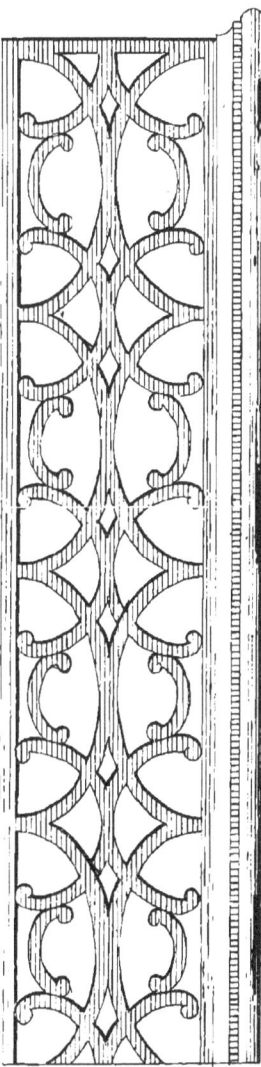

Pl. 10.

Frets proper for Tabernacle Frames

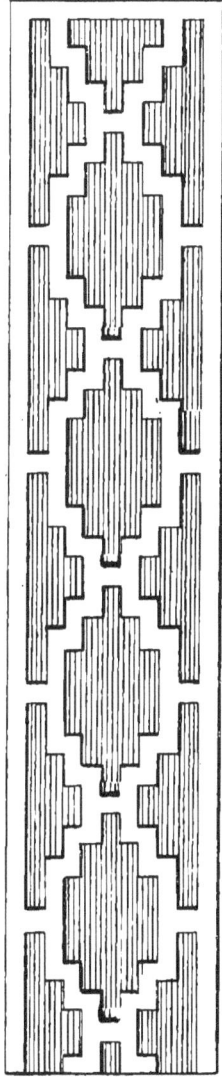

Pl. 11.

A Gothic Fret for Friezes &c

A Chinese Fret proper for Cabinet makers &c

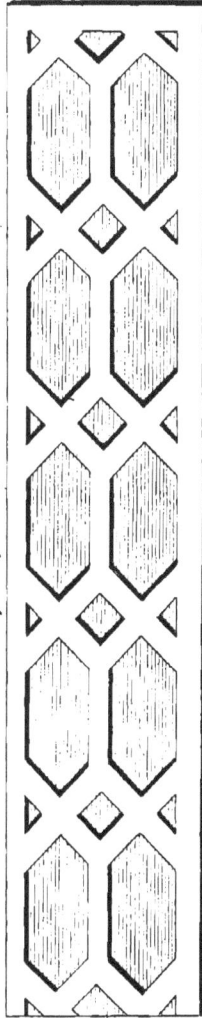

Pl. 12.

Gothic Frets proper for Tabernacle Frames &c

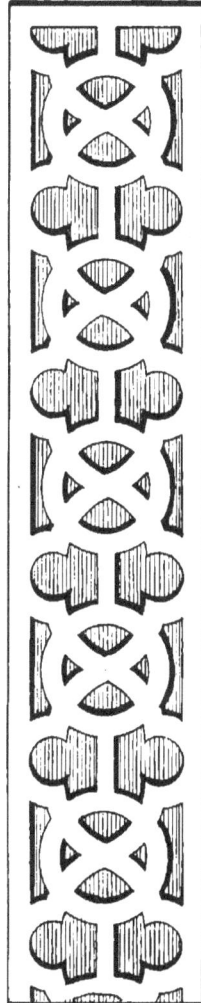

Pl. 13.

Two New Designs of Gothic Frets for Friezes

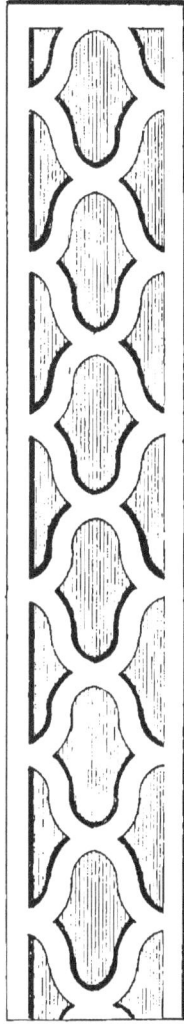

Pl.14.

Two Designs of Gothic Frets for Carpenters &c

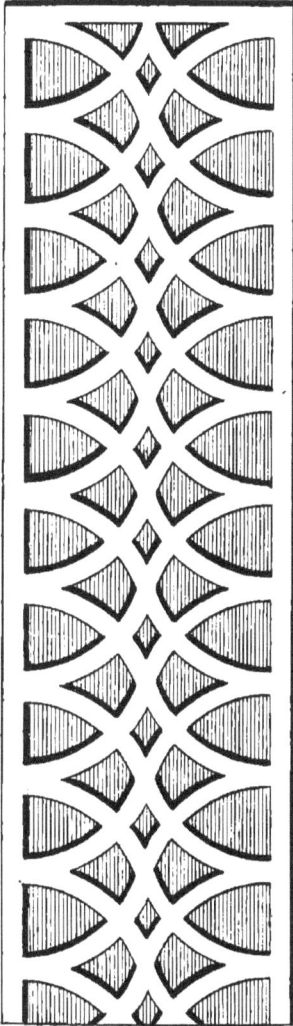

Pl.15.

Gothic Frets proper for Imposts or Architraves

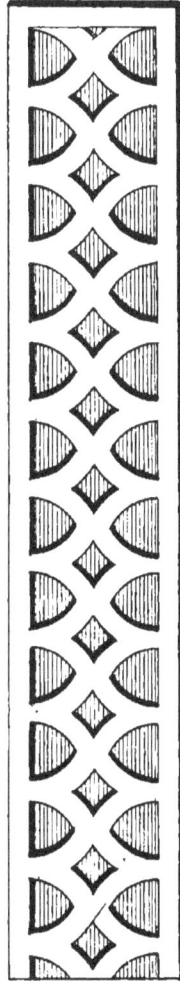

Pl. 16.

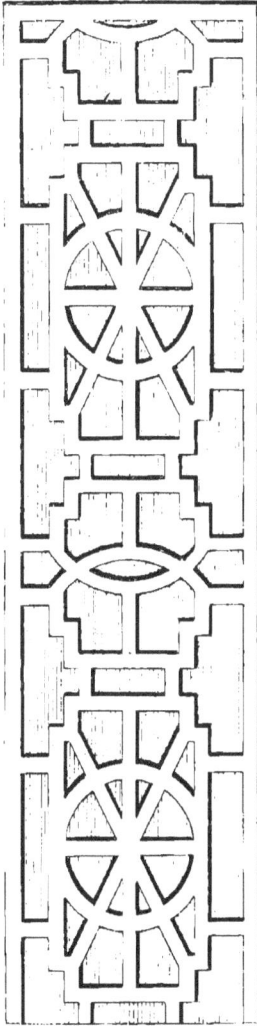

Two Chinese Frets, proper for Tabernacle Frames

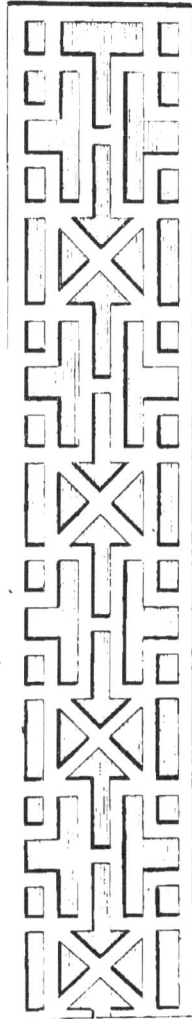

Pl. 17

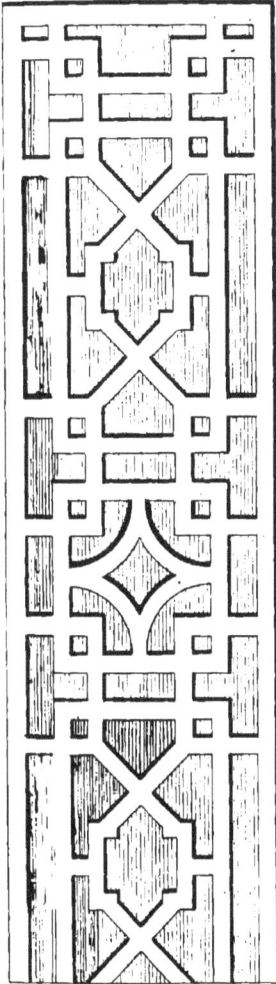

Two Designs of Chinese Frets for Architraves &c

Pl. 18.

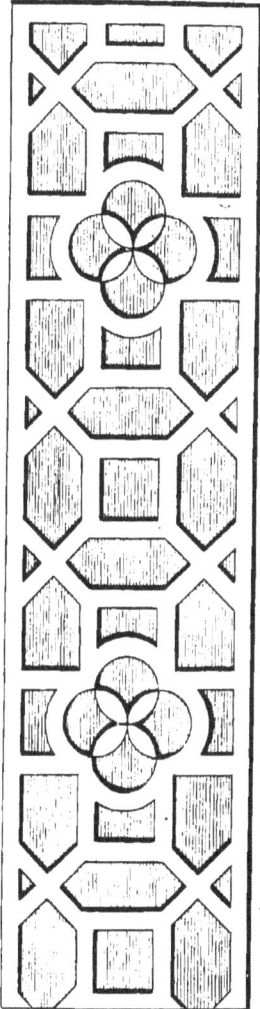

Two New Designs of Frets proper for Imposts

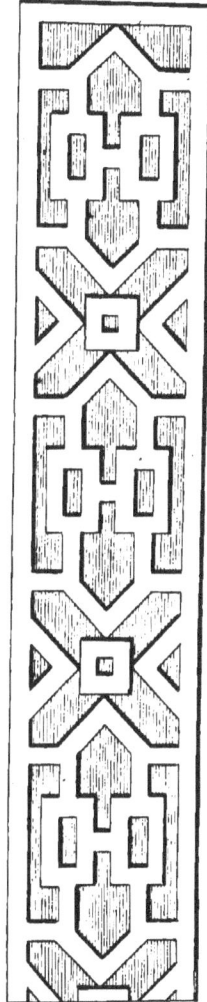

Pl. 19.

Two Chinese Designs of Frets for Friezes &c?

Pl. 20.

A New Design for a Greek Fret

A New Gothic Design for a Fret

Pl. 21.

Two Chinese Frets for Friezes &c

Pl. 22.

Four new Designs for plain and Ornamental Door Tops

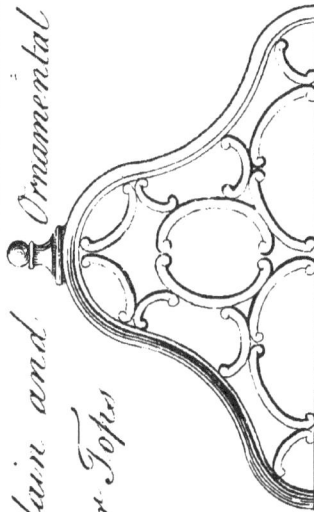

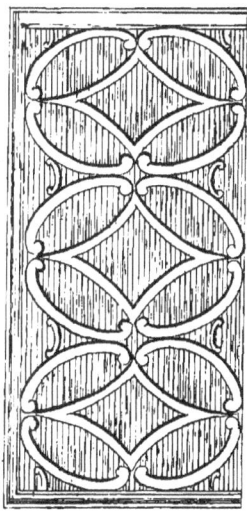

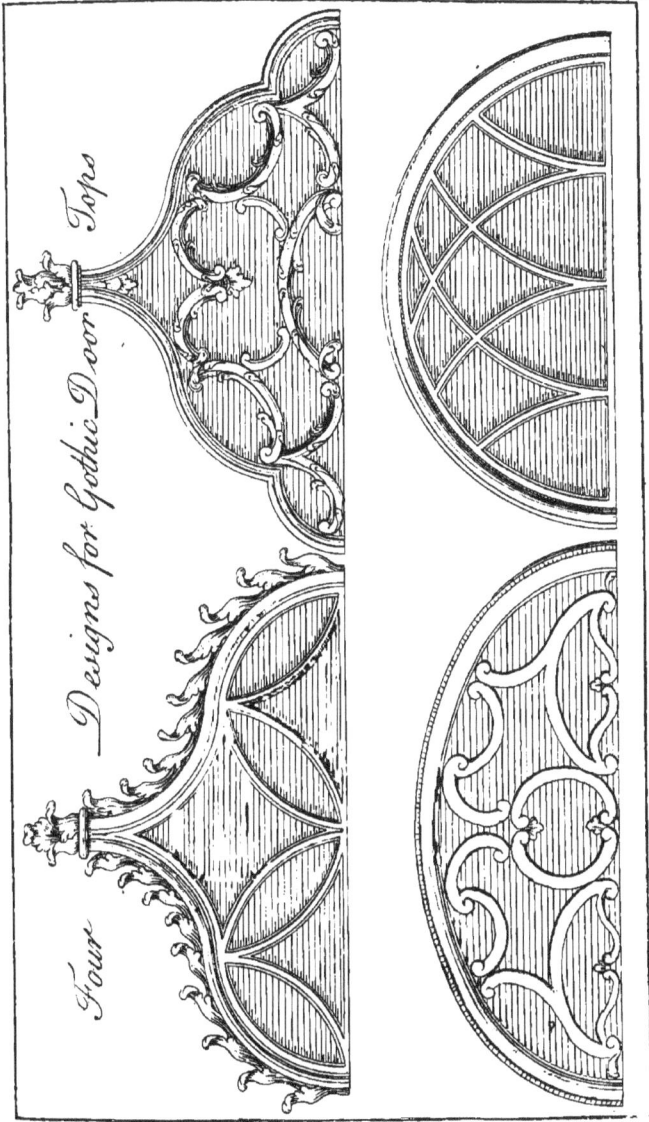

Pl. 23.

Four   Designs for Gothic Door Tops

Pl. 24.

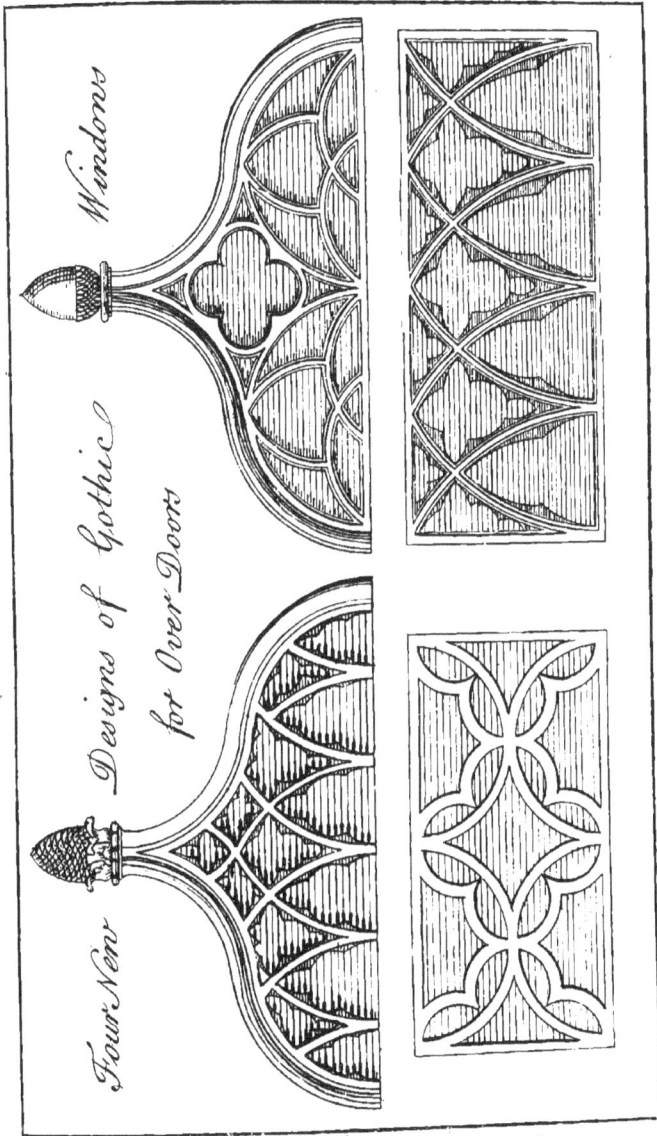

Windows

Designs of Gothic
for Over Doors

Four New

Pl. 25.

Four New Designs for Modern or Ornamental Door Tops

Pl. 26.

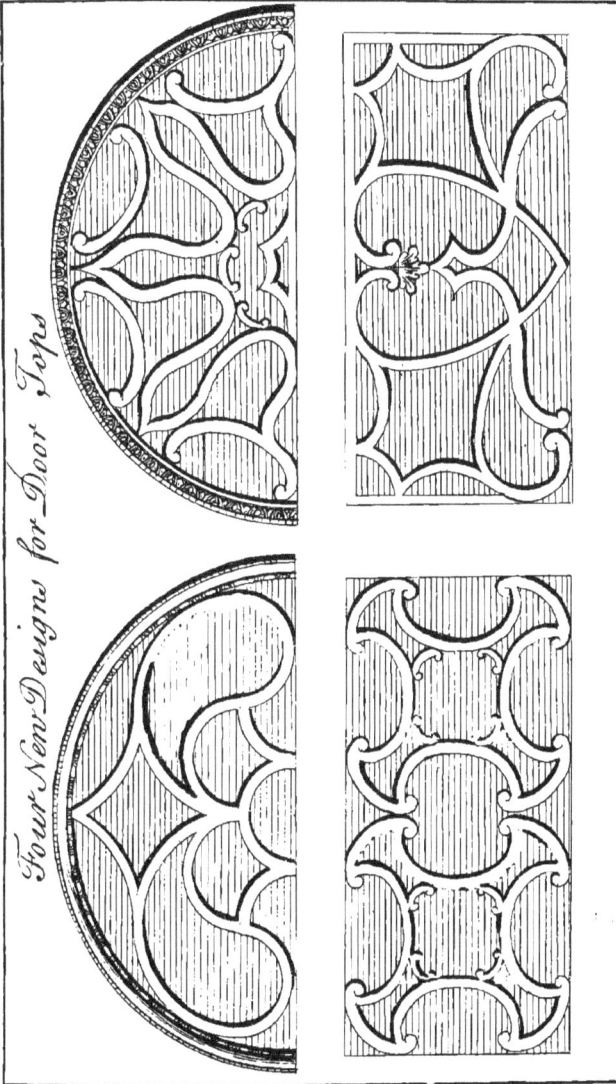

Four New Designs for Door Tops

www.ingramcontent.com/pod-product-compliance
Lightning Source LLC
Chambersburg PA
CBHW021547270326
41930CB00008B/1394